I Wonder W'

Volcanoes Blow Their Tops

and Other Questions About Natural Disasters

Rosie Greenwood

KING*fisher*

KINGFISHER
Kingfisher Publications Plc
New Penderel House
283–288 High Holborn
London WC1V 7HZ
www.kingfisherpub.com

First published by Kingfisher Publications Plc 2004
10 9 8 7 6 5 4 3 2 1

1TR/1103/SHE/RBOW/126.6MA

A CIP catalogue record for this book is available
from the British Library

ISBN: 0 7534 0935 6

Series designer: David West Children's Books
Author: Rosie Greenwood
Consultant: Keith Lye
Illustrations: Mark Bergin 18bl, Peter Dennis (Linda
  Rogers) 16b: Bill Donohoe 24tl, 25r, 26; James Field
  (SGA) 31; Chris Forsey 4bl, 5, 6–7, 8–9, 12–13
  14–15c, 22–23, 24–25c; Mike Lacey (SGA) 14br, 21,
  24l, 27bl, 29r; Simon Mendez 30–31c;
  Roger Stewart 10; Mike Taylor (SGA) 11, 16–17t,
  17br, 18–19t, 19b; Peter Wilkes (SGA) all cartoons.

Printed in Taiwan

CONTENTS

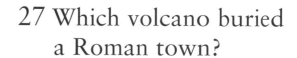

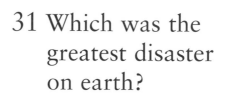

Where does forked lightning come from?

A blinding river of light zigzags through the sky. This is lightning, a giant electrical spark that begins inside towering thunderclouds. Lightning heats the air in its path until it is very hot – hotter than the sun's surface – and the air explodes in a deafening crash of thunder!

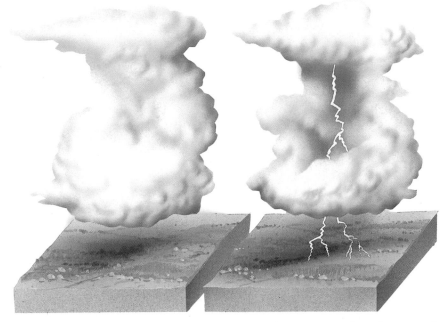

● A thundercloud becomes electrically charged when strong winds toss water droplets, ice crystals and hailstones up and down inside it.

● As the water droplets and ice crystals jostle about, they generate a huge charge of static electricity. This charge is released in brilliant flashes of lightning.

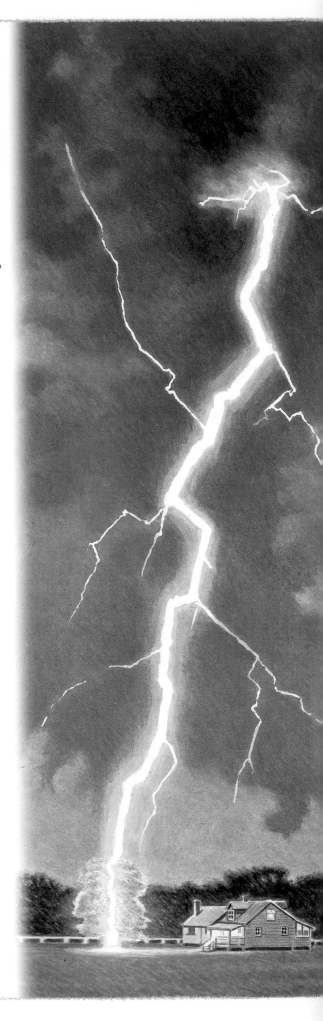

• The Vikings believed that lighting was made by the god Thor hurling his hammer, and that thunder was the rumble of his chariot's wheels.

• If lightning hits sandy ground, the heat can melt the sand. As it cools into a solid again, it forms a glassy sculpture of the lightning flash's path.

What is ball lightning?

Eerie, glowing balls of light are sometimes seen during thunderstorms, floating a little way above the ground. This spooky effect is called ball lightning. Scientists are not sure what causes it, but the balls may be glowing hot gases given off when forked lightning strikes the ground.

• Lightning once struck the Empire State Building in New York, USA, 15 times in 15 minutes!

Why do forests catch fire?

It doesn't take much to start a fire when plants are parched by a hot, rainless summer. A flash of lightning can sometimes spark a dry tree into flame, but most forest fires are caused by people being careless – for example by tossing away a match that is still alight. Fire can burn through a kilometre of forest in an hour, and if a fire rages out of control, it can devastate thousands of hectares of land.

● Indonesian forest fires raged for months in 1997, creating a choking blanket of smoke over much of Southeast Asia.

● Although forest fires can be damaging, some plants need their help to produce new seedlings. Banksias are Australian shrubs whose nutlike seed pods stay tightly shut until triggered open by the heat of a bush fire.

Who bombs fires?

In some countries, firefighters use a specially designed plane to combat fires. The plane can skim over the surface of a lake or the sea and scoop up thousands of litres of water into its tanks. Then the plane flies back to the fire to bomb the flames with its watery load.

● As many as 15,000 bush fires are reported in Australia each year.

How can you fight fire with fire?

A firebreak is a cleared strip of land ahead of a fire, where there's no fuel left to feed the flames. Firefighters sometimes set mini-fires of their own to help clear the ground.

When does a wind become a gale?

The faster the wind blows, the more powerful and dangerous it can be. The Beaufort scale measures wind speed as force 0 to 12 by its effect on the surrounding landscape. A gentle breeze is force 3, for instance – a 12 to 19 km/h wind that rustles twigs. A moderate gale is force 7 – a 50 to 61 km/h wind that makes whole trees sway!

● Force 10 is a whole gale – an 89 to 102 km/h wind that can uproot trees. Storms are force 11, and hurricanes are force 12.

● In March 1993, the eastern coast of Canada and the USA was struck by a savage blizzard carried on hurricane force winds. Thousands of buildings were destroyed or damaged, and the weather was so severe that it was named the Storm of the Century.

Why are blizzards dangerous?

Freezing cold winds can whip up the sudden blinding snowstorms we call blizzards. These can pile up huge snowdrifts, stopping traffic in its tracks and making it impossible for people to go to work or school!

● In 1959, a snowstorm in California, USA, dumped a snowdrift over 4.5 metres deep!

Why did people shoot at clouds?

Hailstones can be the size of cricket balls and can cause enormous damage. In some countries, farmers used to try protecting their crops by firing big guns into clouds to stop the hail. Scientists are unsure if the guns really worked.

● In 1882, in Iowa, USA, two living frogs were found inside big hailstones! They were probably sucked up by a twister.

How much damage can a hurricane do?

With winds roaring at more than 117 km/h, hurricanes are the fiercest storms on earth. They start above warm tropical seas, and if a severe hurricane reaches land, it can flatten forests, smash houses, flip over cars, and even lift boats out of the water!

● Hurricanes can bring torrential rain and crashing waves, and sweep floods of seawater in over the coast. Once on land, the howling winds lose power and quickly die away.

Where is a hurricane's eye?

The eye of a hurricane is a central zone where the wind is fairly calm and there are no big storm clouds. The fast and furious hurricane winds move in a spiral around the eye.

● Each hurricane is given a name. The first of the year usually begins with A, such as Hurricane Alice. The second begins with B, and so on through the alphabet. Few names begin with the letters Q, U, X, Y or Z though!

● Special weather planes help scientists to track hurricanes so they can issue warnings to people.

What do hurricanes, typhoons and cyclones have in common?

They're all words for the same thing – and they all spell trouble! The word 'hurricane' is used in North and South America, 'typhoon' in the Far East, and 'cyclone' in Australia and India.

What wind can sink a ship?

Hurricanes are just as dangerous out at sea as they are on land. Most waves are caused by wind blowing across the water's surface, and a hurricane can whip up a 30-metre-high wall of water. When a freak wave this size smashes down, it can sink even large ships in minutes.

How do sailors know a storm is on its way?

Scientists use planes, ships and satellites to keep a watchful eye on the weather. Information is passed on to the rest of us via TV and radio stations, and sailors make sure they tune in for regular updates.

● Vicious gales and high tides can combine to cause devastating floods in low-lying coastal areas, endangering people and damaging their homes.

Which boats are unsinkable?

Lifeboats race to the rescue during shipwrecks. Modern lifeboats can cope with really wild weather – if a big wave tips one over, it flips back upright!

Why are twisters so dangerous?

'Twister' is a nickname for a tornado, a spinning windstorm that's usually born inside a huge thundercloud. The tornado snakes down to the ground, where it acts like a vacuum cleaner, sucking up everything in its path. Tornadoes are narrower than hurricanes, but they can be just as devastating.

● The world's worst place for tornadoes is Tornado Alley, a narrow belt of land that stretches across several US states.

What is a waterspout?

If a tornado forms over a lake or sea, it sucks up water and is called a waterspout. When its winds die down, it can drop its load of water like a bomb.

- If you're ever caught in a shower of fish, it's because a waterspout has sucked them up from a lake or the sea!

Where can you see a devil?

Hot air will sometimes swirl up from dry desert land, carrying dust and sand more than 150 metres high – this is a dust devil!

Where can wind strip paint off a car?

When a windstorm blows up in the desert, it blasts sand at anything in its path. Sand can strip the surface from all sorts of tough materials – even cars. That's why wood is smoothed with sandpaper and stone is polished with sandblasting machines!

● A sprinkling of sand from the Sahara Desert has been known to fall in Britain, thousands of kilometres away.

What is the Dust Bowl?

The Dust Bowl is a region in the USA's Midwest whose name dates back to the 1930s. There was so little rain in those years that the soil dried to dust and was blown away by windstorms. No crops grew, and farming families had to abandon their land and homes.

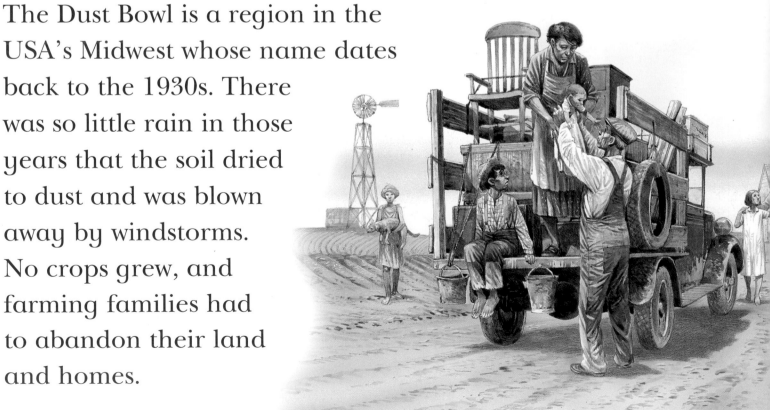

● Ancient rock paintings show that the Sahara was once far wetter and greener, and that giraffes and elephants grazed there.

How can a child be so destructive?

●La Niña has the opposite effect to El Niño. In Australia and Indonesia, for example, La Niña brings rain and good conditions for farming.

Warm and cold ocean currents help to shape the world's climate. In the Pacific Ocean, a cold current called La Niña (Spanish for 'the girl') usually flows west from South America to Indonesia. But every three to seven years, a warm current called El Niño ('the boy') flows eastwards in the opposite direction instead. Sometimes El Niño is strong, causing disastrous weather, including droughts, hurricanes and floods, from Alaska to Australia.

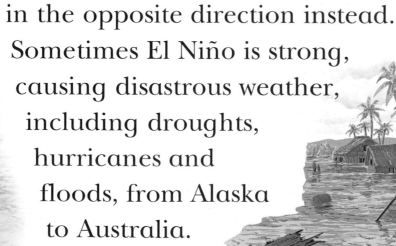

When does mud slide?

If torrentially heavy rain pelts down onto a steep mountain slope, it can turn loose soil into liquid mud and wash it away. Sometimes, a roaring river of mud sweeps down off the mountain, drowning everything in its path.

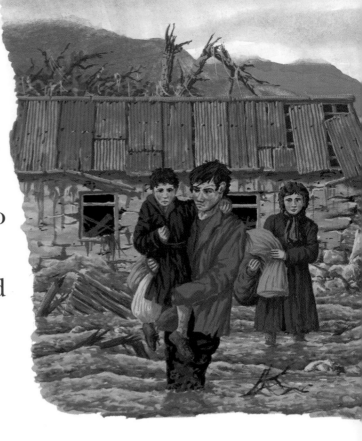

● The waters rose incredibly quickly when flash floods struck southern Mozambique in February 2000. There was so little time to escape that thousands of people were trapped for days on house roofs and in treetops.

What makes floods happen in a flash?

Flash floods got their name because they happen so quickly. Torrential rain can swamp a river or stream, making it suddenly burst its banks and spill out over the surrounding countryside.

● When a Colombian volcano blew its top in 1985, the heat melted its icecap and created mudflows called lahars which buried a whole town.

● Lahars can surge downhill at almost 100 km/h.

● Noah's Flood may have happened when the Mediterranean Sea broke through a strip of land, turning a freshwater lake into the salty Black Sea.

How do floods help?

When rivers burst their banks, they dump rich mud on the land which helps farmers to grow crops. The ancient Egyptians, for example, built their great civilization on the narrow strip of fertile farming land created by the River Nile flooding every year. The rest of their huge country was dry, dusty desert.

When does snow race at 300 km/h?

Snow can break away from a mountain slope and crash downhill at breakneck speed. This is an avalanche, and it can be triggered by anything from an earthquake to the swish of a skier's skis. The worst avalanches race along as fast as an express train, roaring louder than thousands of lions, as they bury homes and villages, railways and roads.

● Watch where you yodel in Switzerland – loud noises are another way of setting off an avalanche!

● During World War I, soldiers fired their guns to set avalanches off on their enemies.

Who is an avalanche victim's best friend?

No avalanche rescue team would be complete without its specially trained dogs. With their keen sense of smell, dogs are brilliant at sniffing out people hidden under the snow. And as soon as they find someone, the dogs start digging a rescue tunnel.

What makes land slide?

Disasters, such as avalanches and landslides, are most common in mountainous regions where there are no trees. Trees help keep land safe because they bury their roots down into the ground, anchoring it and stopping it from being swept away.

What happens in an earthquake?

A small earthquake makes the ground tremble. A powerful one makes it shudder and shake like a ship rocking on the ocean, and even crack wide open. The most devastating earthquakes can move mountains, make rivers change course, and bring entire cities tumbling down to the ground.

● In Japanese legend, earthquakes were triggered by a giant catfish called Namazu wriggling about.

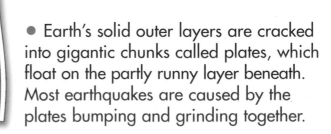

● Earth's solid outer layers are cracked into gigantic chunks called plates, which float on the partly runny layer beneath. Most earthquakes are caused by the plates bumping and grinding together.

When does soil turn into soup?

In areas with soft, wet soil, an earthquake can sometimes make the ground act like it's a liquid. Buildings sink, and stay firmly stuck even when the shaking stops and the ground becomes solid again.

● Laser beams are used to measure ground movement and help warn when an earthquake is coming.

How do we measure earthquakes?

An instrument called a seismometer is used to measure the vibrations, or shaking movements, of the ground in an earthquake. In some seismometers, a pen records the vibrations on paper wrapped around a turning drum. The pen is fixed to a weight and stays still during the quake, while the drum bounces about.

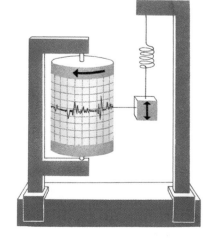

Which mountains spit fire?

If you ever see huge fiery clouds spurting out of a mountain, you can be sure it's a volcano – and what's worse, it's blowing its top! The most violent volcanoes explode like bombs, spitting out clouds of hot ash, chunks of solid rock, and fountains of the runny rock we call lava.

Why do volcanoes blow their tops?

Deep beneath a violent volcano is a vast chamber. Hot runny rock and gases build up here until they blast upwards under immense pressure through cracks in the earth's crust.

● Scientists who study volcanoes are called vulcanologists, after Vulcan, the Roman god of fire.

Where can you see rivers of rock?

Sometimes a red-hot river of lava pours out of a volcano and flows down its sides. The runny rock can reach temperatures of over 1,000°C – much, much hotter than an oven – and flow faster than you can run!

● As if volcanoes weren't dangerous enough, their ash clouds can become electrically charged and produce lightning!

What is an avalanche of ash?

Volcanic ash can be even more dangerous than lava. Sometimes ash clouds are not thrown up into the air, but roll down over the sides of a volcano like an avalanche. As they race downhill, these scorching-hot ash clouds burn, boil or melt everything in their path.

● Violent volcanoes can affect earth's climate, by throwing up ash clouds that shut out the sun's light. The eruption of Indonesia's Mount Tambora in 1815, for example, was followed by worldwide bad weather.

● When Mount Pinatubo in the Philippines erupted in 1991, an avalanche of ash destroyed land as far as 17 kilometres away.

Which volcano buried a Roman town?

When Italy's Mount Vesuvius erupted in August CE79, ash fell like snow over the Roman town of Pompeii, burying it in 6-metre-deep drifts. Then it rained. Afterwards the ash set like concrete, freezing the town in time until it was first excavated in the 1860s.

● Despite its chilly name, Iceland is a real hot spot with hundreds of volcanoes – lava has even set houses on fire!

How can volcanoes be good for you?

Although volcanic ash can be so destructive, it brings benefits as well. As the ash weathers down, it enriches the soil and helps farmers to grow bumper harvests.

How big can waves get?

When an average tsunami wave reaches the shore, it rears up into a 20-metre-high monster. But the tallest in modern times was 85 metres high – almost as high as the Statue of Liberty in New York City Harbor!

● Tsunamis can speed across the ocean at 1,000 km/h – as fast as a jet plane!

● A tsunami may have played a major role in the mysteriously sudden end of the Minoan civilization on the Greek island of Crete around 3,500 years ago. Gigantic 40-metre-high waves are thought to have smashed into Crete at that time, wiping out coastal towns and the entire Minoan fleet.

What sets off tsunamis?

Unlike ordinary ocean waves, which are mainly whipped up by the wind blowing over the water's surface, most tsunamis are shocked into life on the ocean floor. Underwater earthquakes, landslides and volcanic eruptions are all violent enough to kick-start a tsunami.

● When a volcano blew the Indonesian island of Krakatau apart in 1883, so much rock was hurled into the sea that tsunami waves were set off. The monster waves even picked up a ship and dumped it in the jungle on the nearby island of Sumatra.

What is dangerous about space rocks?

Earth is under constant attack from space rocks. Most are no bigger than a pebble and burn up as they plunge through the air. But every now and then, a big rock smashes into the ground and blasts out a hole called a crater.

● Space rocks that hit the ground are called meteorites.

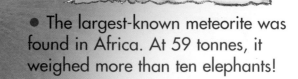

● The largest-known meteorite was found in Africa. At 59 tonnes, it weighed more than ten elephants!

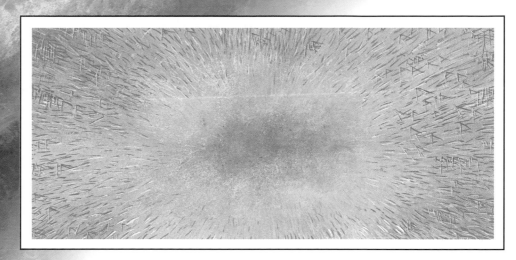

● When a huge space rock exploded high above Siberia in 1908, it flattened a city-sized area of forest on the ground below.

Which was the greatest disaster on earth?

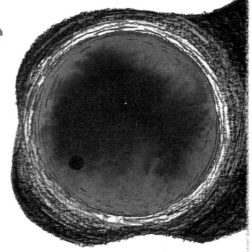

Many scientists think a massive meteorite strike killed off the dinosaurs 65 million years ago. The blast blew up enough dust to block out the sun's rays for months. Without sunlight, plants died. Cold and hunger killed off the plant-eating dinosaurs first, and then the meat-eaters.

● One day the sun will swell into a red giant star and boil away earth's life-giving water. Don't worry, though, this won't happen for another 5 billion years.

Index

A
aircraft 7, 11, 12
ancient Egypt 19
ash, volcanic 24, 25, 26–27
avalanche 20–21

B
ball lightning 5
Beaufort scale 8
blizzard 8, 9
bush fire 6–7

C
climate 17, 26
crater 30
crust, earth's 22, 24
current, ocean 17
cyclone see hurricane

D
desert 15, 16
dinosaurs 31
dog, rescue 21
drought 16, 17
Dust Bowl 16
dust devil 15

E
earthquake 20, 22–23, 29
El Niño 17
electricity 4
Empire State Building 5, 28
eye of hurricane 11

F
farming 9, 16, 17, 19, 27
fire 6–7
firefighter 7
flash flood 18
flood 10, 13, 17, 18–19
forest fire 6–7
friction 4

G
gale 8, 13

H
hailstones 4, 9
hurricane 8, 10–11, 12, 14, 17

K
Krakatau 29

L
La Niña 17
lahar 19
landslide 21, 29
laser 23
lava 24, 25
lifeboat 13
lightning 4–5, 6, 25

M
meteorite 30–31
Minoans 28
Mozambique 18
mudflow see lahar
mudslide 18

N
Noah's Flood 19

P
Pinatubo, Mount 26
Pompeii 27

R
rain 10, 17, 18
  see also drought
River Nile 19
Romans 24, 27

S
Sahara Desert 16, 17
sailors 12
sand 5, 15, 16
satellite 12
seismometer 23
ships 12–13
snow 9, 20–21
space rocks 30–31
storm 4–5, 8–19
Storm of the Century 8
sun 4, 26, 31

T
Tambora, Mount 26
Thor 5
thunder 4, 5
thundercloud 4, 14
tornado 14
Tornado Alley 14
trees 6–7, 8, 21
tsunami 28–29
twister see tornado
typhoon see hurricane

V
Vesuvius, Mount 27
Vikings 5
volcano 19, 24–27, 29
vulcanologist 24

W
waterspout 14
waves, ocean 10, 12–13, 28–29
wind 4, 8–16